..what
Employers
WANT.

Bunmi Akingbade

If a man is called to be a street sweeper, he should sweep the street even as Michelangelo painted, or Beethoven composed music or Shakespeare wrote poetry. He should sweep streets so well that all the hosts of heaven and earth will pause to say here lived a great street sweeper who did his Job well.

Martin Luther King Jr

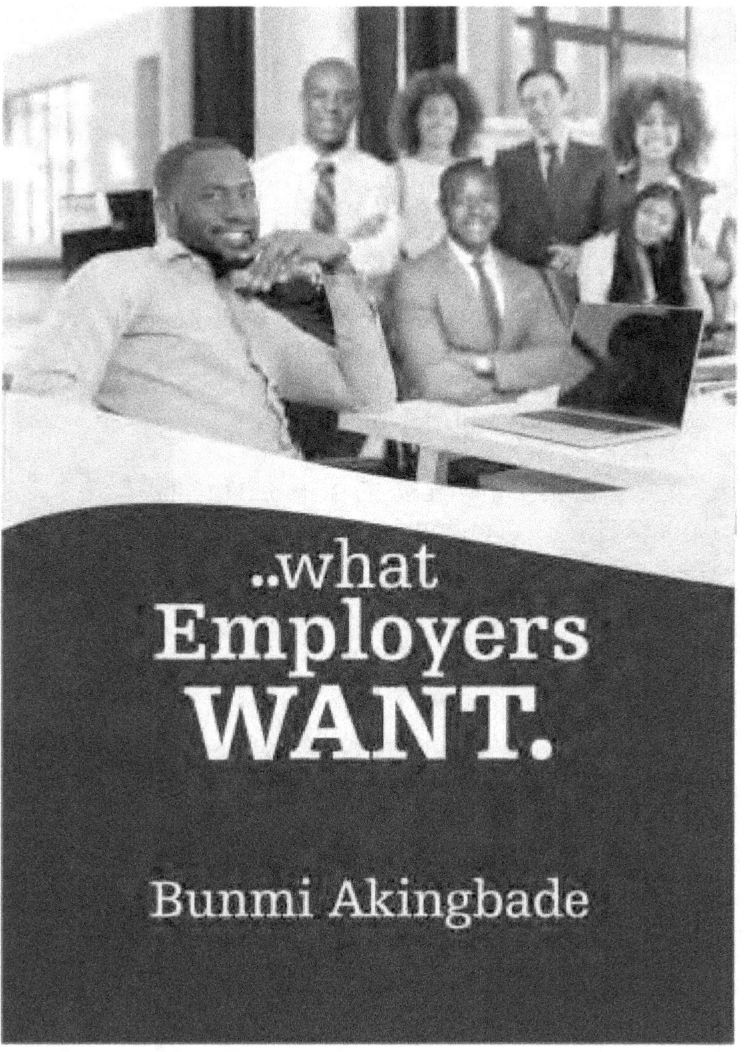

..what
Employers
WANT.

Bunmi Akingbade

Printed in Nigeria by Diamond Media:
diamondtfi2@gmail.com
08064281007

For more Enquiries Call:
08030760831, 08033325735, 08153717008
Email: Lacare247@gmail.com
Facebook: Lacare innovative and creativity
Twitter: @Lacare247
Instagram: @Lacare247

Content

Introduction

INTRODUCTION

Most graduates are eager to get a Job immediately after school or when the need arises. However, searching for the right Job could be demanding. Once you get the Job you need to immediately add value to the organization, you are not employed because you need a job rather you are employed to meet a need in the organization and to add value to the organization.

Employers want employees, who can demonstrate the required skills needed to succeed on the job, add value to the organization and take it to the next level. They want to see a high level of dependability on your side, which involves you taking personal ownership of all aspects of the Job including; being on time, dressing well, working in a professional manner, being proactive, hardworking, creating value, bringing solutions, exhibiting leadership skills, thinking outside the box, having industry-specific skills and demonstrating a high level commitment and integrity.

This book provides the crucial foundation required for employees to excel at the workplace and know what is expected from them. It also provides basic understanding to support employees give their best to their employer at all times.

It explains further insights to help you excel on the Job. Understanding what employers want will ultimately smoothen your journey to the top and help you remain relevant in the workplace. It will also help you maintain a good perception and acceptance in the heart of your employer. It is a must read.

Bunmi Akingbade

Chapter 1

The Job Search

...The right time to prepare
for a job is not when you have it,
you need to prepare for it before it
comes. Ask yourself, "do I have
what it takes to perform effectively
when I get the Job?" "Do I have
the required skills needed to
succeed on the Job?"...

Congratulations! You are so excited you are done with school; you are now responsible for yourself. The Job search begins; you are hoping to get a promising and rewarding dream job so you can start earning a living.

Searching for a Job can be hard work; it takes lots of time, patience and efforts. You put your Curriculum Vitae together, spend time searching for job vacancies online and offline, you fill out application forms and prepare for interviews. Sometimes no matter how hard you try, you feel you are not getting anywhere because it is the same story! We are not hiring.

You speak to friends, look for job links and those who can link you up, you attend various interviews; send your Curriculum Vitae all over the place. You apply to numerous organizations, you are invited for interviews; you get so excited! Sadly, they inform you the position has been taken! the Job search you thought was over starts all over again.

Some job seekers decide to make ends meet while searching for a Job, they go on to learn and acquire vocational skills such as fashion designing, hair styling, make up, event planning, electrical repairs, Arts and Crafts and the likes. Some go into Forex trading while others go into buying and selling just to keep body and soul together while still searching for their dream job.

There is pressure in the Labor market cause you are not the only one in need of a Job; there are several job seekers at every interview. You feel the need to keep hope alive, believe in yourself, you are hopeful the search will soon be over. Some employers require you write a test; having done this, you are invited for an interview. You look forward to hearing good news, sadly all you hear is: "Thank you for attending the interview, we regret to inform you the interview was not successful." You go through series of emotions again and again. Some organizations simply would not respond, they keep you anxiously waiting for nothing; you eventually give up on them.

As a succor, some Job seekers decide to become entrepreneurs instead of wasting productive years in the labor market. They take a decision that life must go on; they become entrepreneurs by situation not by choice.

Those who stay in the labor market know searching for a Job can be very demanding; everyone you come across know you are looking for a Job, just incase they have useful information that can change your situation.

Eventually, you secure a job with an employer who is ready to hire you subject to negotiation, however the final offer may not interest you but you feel you do not have a choice because if you do not take this offer you are not sure when the next Job opportunity will present itself.
Many employers take undue advantage of the situation, which is unethical. Other employers have ethical standards of making an offer based on competence rather than desperation of an employee.

Congratulations! You finally get the job, it could be your dream Job, a "let me manage it" Job or, a job for the meantime. Whatever the case; you are now employed. Your prayer has finally been answered. You are out of the Labor Market for now or for good.

You are excited Life is good! You tell family and friends you now have a job. What a wonderful feeling; finally, an end has come to your Job search; you can now start earning a living.

You look forward to possibilities of moving higher and higher on the Job while others keep searching for better Job openings once they gain the required experience. Some employees continue their search for a better Job while working on the current one.

In a bid to get something better as soon as possible, some even go as far as giving their Curriculum Vitae to their employer's client while on duty. Nothing could be more unethical. Some feel the job is not worth it at all, considering the pay. "How much are they paying me" is a common parlance from the lips of most employees. No matter the amount, be grateful and keep your focus on what your employer wants.
Congratulations you have a Job, it's time to play your role and deliver your part of the contract. In reality some people may still be searching for work, stay positive the search will soon be over. Whatever level you are presently this book reveals what employers wants and how to achieve it with a view to honoring God, your employer and yourself as you give your best to the job with the right attitude, motive and behavior, you are destined for the Top.

The right time to prepare for a job is not when you have it, you need to prepare for it before it comes. Ask yourself, "do I have what it takes to perform effectively when I get the Job?" "Do I have the required skills needed to succeed on the Job?" Bear in mind you have been employed to achieve result for your organization and solve problems, how prepared are you for this? You need to have the skills required to enable you perform exceptionally well on the Job when the opportunity arises. Remember you are hired to deliver value to your organization.

As an employee you create value for and also extract value from your organization. Remember you don't work only for a salary but also for your Personal Development (Value) you can get from the Job.

You need to be accountable, accountability is taking ownership and responsibility for something, agreeing to see it through and solve any problems along the way. Accountability means taking ownership of your role.

Build yourself to be a great communicator, motivator and decision maker, be a visionary employee able to see the big picture. Don't just look at what is in front of you but look out for possibilities. Determine your abilities, manage yourself well, regulate your time, attention and emotions. Be aware of your strengths, weaknesses and potentials. Show compassion; maintain self-control and discipline in your actions. Be forward thinking, open minded and flexible.

Chapter 2
Driving Productivity
...You are recruited to solve
problems. The number one focus
when you resume is to ensure you
achieve maximum productivity for
your employer. You have been
selected from many, therefore, you
need to display you have what it
takes to get the Job done...

You are recruited to solve problems. The number one focus when you resume is to ensure you achieve maximum productivity for your employer. You have been selected from many, therefore, you need to display you have what it takes to get the Job done.

It may not be your dream Job, however, having accepted the terms and conditions of the Job, your priority should be focused on achieving productivity that drives the results your employer wants to see.

Having employed you, your employer wants value. Value comes by having a growth mindset towards the Job, be ready to take the company from the current level to the next level, be disciplined and dedicated to the Job, ensure you have the right expertise to perform effectively on the Job. Be informed, prepared, smart, safe and ready.

Your job is an opportunity to make an impact, be purposeful, ensure what needs to happen gets done the right way; bearing in mind you are there to make a difference.

Some employees spend as little as six months, sometimes as much as thirty-five years on a Job leaving behind either regrettable or remarkable memories. Think about what you want to be remembered for when you are no longer on the Job. Focus on adding value, make an impact and not just to earn an income. Make it a time to learn, give your best and gain experience while on the Job. Be willing to learn new things and improve on the Job.

Whenever there is a problem, think solution. Don't leave it to your employer, add value, display problem solving skills, see yourself not just as an employee but a partner in progress, give your best even without getting the best pay, don't join in the popular parlance; "How much are they even paying me." Remember your life is what you create it to be. Be productive, be a person who is passionate about success and value.

Learn to consistently improve yourself on the Job, influence other employees in the workplace positively. It is not a time to criticize your boss or announce over and over how you hate your Job, the salary, the customers, the environment etc. Rather give your best to your employer, be a role model, make an impact on the Job, be an asset not a liability to your employer. Be strategically creative, apply yourself to the Job, add value, do more than you are paid for. Be productive in the workplace.

An ideal employee displays productivity by doing things faster, doing things right, producing strategic results, removing hurdles, displays creative thinking and provides solutions to issues.

Employees are required to understand the nature of their job and have complete knowledge of the business. You need to understand what to do to advance the company's goal and vision.

Employee's effort, determination, skills and experience contribute to success in the workplace. Be bold to make a difference, execute with excellence, and champion productivity.

No employer wants to hire a liability. Be ready to learn fast on the Job, maximize your potentials, be the right staff to your employer, add value to the organization, be productive, achieve results, be dependable and responsible.

In driving productivity, communication skill is required. You cannot go far on the Job if you do not have the ability to communicate well with others. Most problems that occur in the workplace could be resolved with proper communication in place.

Employers value communication skill because it allows one to mitigate risk and avoid problems before they arise. Having strong communication skills help drive productivity in the workplace.

Employees must learn to work with others; the importance of teamwork cannot be overstated. In every level, one will be required to collaborate with others internally or externally. You must be friendly and easy to get along with.

In driving productivity employees must understand how to examine information objectively to determine the best way to move forward. Employees are bound to run into unexpected challenges and setbacks; however, employees should be able to take action and find creative solutions to problems.

Employees should understand it is not about being busy, but about being productive. Results must be clear. Employees must take responsibility for driving productivity relentlessly and take all related processes, training, personal development necessary to enhance productivity serious. Employers value employees who stay committed and remain focused on driving productivity.

Productivity is not about having thousands or millions of staff but rather working with few who can THINK and INNOVATE STRATEGICALLY.

Productive employees always set their goals first, they don't just know what to do they know why they do it. They have short term and long-term goals. Productive employees have purpose, which informs everything they do.

A productive employee is indispensable to the organization's success. They are dedicated, organized and consistent on any given task.

Productive employees waste zero mental energy worrying about what might happen to them, they put all their efforts into making things happen. Productive employees find it easy to build in time and opportunity to experience new things.

Productivity means producing valuable and quality work in a short amount of time, creating value with less resource; meaning doing more with less.

The more productive you are the more valuable you are to your organization bearing in mind productivity is never an accident. It is always the result of commitment to excellence, intelligent planning, and focused effort according to Paul J. Meyer.

Chapter 3

Focus on Reality

...There are certain behaviors
required from employees. Being
ready, available and willing to get
the job done, desires to go above
and beyond normal duty routine to
bring further success to the
organization...

Punctuality is the Soul of business. Employers expect employees to be punctual at all times, if you need to be absent or late you must notify your boss or the appropriate hierarchy immediately. Punctual and available employees provide peace of mind. Being punctual shows your level of responsibility, value for time, adherence to procedures and respect for your employer.

There are certain behaviors required from employees. Being ready, available and willing to get the job done, desires to go above and beyond normal duty routine to bring further success to the organization.

Being courteous and friendly to coworkers, managers and customers are values to hold in high priority. Such employees make office life more pleasant than those who seek to cause disturbances and drama. Employees should have the ability to express self with clarity and comportment, which includes mannerisms, composure, appearance and poise.

Employees should have task –oriented behaviors displayed at work such as being active, always busy with something and ready to be engaged, positively ambitious, has strong quest for success, cautious, being very careful to avoid errors and very creative. Someone who can make up things easily or has new ideas, always ready to think outside the box.

Employers want employees who meet deadlines, gladly take responsibilities and tells the truth. Employees who are honest and earnestly explains an oversight or mistake. Such employees values integrity.

Corruption is frowned at in the workplace, corrupt employees are never appreciated cause they affect the workplace negatively. The difference between a corrupt person and an honest person is that a corrupt person has a price while the honest person has value. Honest employees are valued in the workplace.

If you think like the owner of the business you will make right decisions. Employees should never be involved in any type of fraud in the workplace, model the right behavior. Be honest, self driven and motivated. There is a saying; "if you control yourself your Glory will appear". You need to be morally successful, high on integrity and character.

Understand the specific Job description, competence and proficiency level expected on the role. Know the impact your Job has to the success of the organization. Constantly learn and develop yourself, read books, attend relevant trainings, be informed. Constantly strive to improve yourself.

Success in the workplace depends largely on you and what you make of opportunities that present itself. Seek help when you need it and extend help to others.
Connect, be informed and develop to be the best version of yourself. Never fail to achieve your God given potential in life. Have a Positive mindset regardless of what you experience on the job; it will always get better. Your job should excite you. Follow instructions and personally seek opportunities to develop the workplace.

Be excellent at your work so skilled, so sharp; have a great attitude that will stand you out among others. Distinguish yourself, be willing to do more and give extra than you're paid for. Come up higher and succeed.

Be an employee who takes on challenges of personal development and learning very serious. Employees must be fully present at work as thinking, imaginative and innovative individuals.

Employees are expected to demonstrate thinking skills, mental flexibility, ability to solve problems and create value. Employees need to align their conduct with the values of the organization.

Organizations have zero tolerance to fraud. Avoid employee fraud and misconduct. Adhere to the guidelines of expected behavior in the workplace. Exercise your duty with care and diligence. Employees should display high-level commitment, focus on achieving results, be proactive and maximize your potential.
 Knowledge is power: employees need to acquire knowledge, knowledge empowers you. It is the accumulation of facts and information, which is a key factor to man's success in the race of life. To be informed is to be transformed. Having the right knowledge in the workplace sets you up for success when in doubt do not be afraid to ask question. Have a personal journey to greatness strategy.

There are three types of people the Proactive, Passive and reactive. Employers want to hire proactive people for their organizational growth and profitability of the business.

Employers want to hire employees who foster creativity, team building, manage complexity, drive results and innovation.

Employers appreciate employees who display great code of ethics, understand associated behaviors expected of them in the workplace, pursue integrity and promote ethical behavior.

Employees are required to carefully consider their actions in the workplace, be honest, accountable, and understand the potential consequence of both positive and negative decisions.

Employees should take up the role of a leader on the job, think ahead, plan for the future, exhaust all possibilities, envision problems and dream up solutions to them. Employees are expected to have the ability to transform vision and strategy into reality, be flexible and open.

Success of an organization is vital; hiring the right employee is critical such employee must thereby have a sound character, good habits and the right attitude.

Chapter 4

Getting Fired

...Employees who do not meet
expectations of employers over
time can get fired...

Employees who do not meet expectations of employers over time can get fired. Some of the reasons for these are when employees are not performing to expectations on the job for which they were hired.

Poor performance is one of the most frequently cited reasons why employees get fired. No employer fires a productive employee, when employees move too slow, make too many errors, do not meet defined performance standards, ask too many irrelevant questions, miss deadlines, lack a sense of urgency, use poor judgment or seems not to care about important issues to the organization such employees stands a good chance of getting fired.

When employees take too much time off work without valid reasons, arrive late to work despite several cautions, steals from employer, play games on the internet during office hours or watch videos, check out Facebook, gossip and bad mouth. These are not benefitting behaviors in the workplace and could get one fired.

Fraud, corruption and mismanagement of resources are certain to attract not only being fired, but also being jailed and ruining a lifetime career. Such behavior should be completely avoided.

Conducting personal business while at work on employer's time is unethical. Every employer has the expectation that when an employee shows up for work they will put in agreed hours. This does not happen because some employees are busy running their own personal business or looking for another job, going for several interviews on employer's time, some are busy conducting a side business and taking too many personal calls while at work. Such employees stand a high chance of getting fired.

Dishonesty and lying on the Job; such as falsifying company records, falsifying expense reports, lying to the boss, falsifying records on Curriculum Vitae just to get a job can also get one fired. Integrity is key

Employees who do not get along with others are poor team players; always putting up bad attitudes in the work place stands a chance of getting fired to avoid influencing others negatively on the job. Employees need to focus their efforts on what matters most.

Employers need to discuss observed negative behaviors in the workplace with employees and expect positive changes, such discussion could be documented. Meetings can be organized where work performance and failure to meet expected standard of performance is reviewed and discussed with employees. However, where an employee still displays such negative behavioral trend, reality is such employee will most likely get fired considering the purpose of hiring was not achieved.

Employers appreciate employees who are well behaved, always ready to take action, employees who value innovation and creativity and want the company to get better, employees who display leadership, responsibility and accountability.

Employees must put in their best to avoid been fired on the Job. The Labour Market is already saturated.

Chapter 5

Committed to Serve

...Employees commitment is the
attachment an employee has on
the job due to their experiences; it
can indicate the level of
satisfaction, and engagement
among employees...

...Employees should understand it
is not about being busy, but about
being productive. Results must be
clear...

33

Employees must display commitment to serve, dedicate yourself to the Job. See your Job as a gift; figure out new ways to accomplish tasks. Be committed to giving your best to your employer. See yourself as a Team player; be productive, loyal and committed to the organization. Team players display willingness to collaborate with others in order to accomplish goals.

Do not focus on how much your employer is paying, but on the value you are adding to the Job. Is the organization better off with you on board? Some employees keep changing jobs every three to six months, always looking for greener pastures, never satisfied; forgetting that greener pastures come through service.

Employees should work to learn not to earn especially at the initial stage; in due time you will be an irreplaceable employee dictating your terms and condition, but for now stay focused on the job, learn and be committed to serve.

Commitment from employees show employee as being dependable and responsible; being dependable means you do what you say you will do. Employers value employees who come to work on time, take responsibility for their actions and behaviors, such employees value their job, they know expectations and required performance level of their employer.
Employees must take pride in their work and ensure it is done well and thoroughly. Employees must always try to improve one's skill and increase value while serving as a role model to others in the workplace.

Employees commitment is the attachment an employee has on the job due to their experiences; it can indicate the level of satisfaction, and engagement among employees.

Committed workers are highly desirable because they remain faithful regardless of the situation in the company. They buy into the vision of the workplace no matter the level of the job. Every job is relevant: a cleaning job, security job, Petrol attendant, administrative work, teaching, consultant, marketing etc. Every salary-paying job is very important to your employer and to God who provided the Job in the first place.

Committed employees buy into the vision of the workplace; they do their job diligently, pay attention to time, communicate effectively, share information, make decisions, stick with them and give good feedback.

Committed employees make conscious effort to explore, investigate and learn without needing an external person to persuade them. They are self-driven, focused and responsible for their Personal development.

Employers are always on the look out for committed, hard working employees who use their initiatives and are proactive about finding new ways to help at work. Employees who use their initiatives do not wait around for their boss to assign them tasks and responsibilities. They are self motivated and driven to do whatever they can to move their company to the next Level.

Loyal employees not only work for their pay, but are committed to the success of the company. More often than not, they put the company's interest ahead of their own and are always striving to improve themselves and their role.

It is important employees are committed and loyal: do your job well, take pride in your work, never stop learning and advancing in your field.

Commitment is one of the best drivers of leadership; leadership is vital to any organization. Commitment to work can be defined as the level of enthusiasm an employee has towards tasks assigned at the workplace. It is the feeling of responsibility that a person has towards the goals, mission and vision of the organization he or she is associated with.

The success or failure of an organization is closely related to the effort and motivation of its employees. Motivation of employees is often the product of their commitment towards the job.
Committed employees are in high demand because they work hard, are consistent and passionate about the job, they keep things in balance and are high on integrity. You don't see them jumping ship at every chance they get. Committed employers don't give in to fraud in the workplace; they have no business committing fraud and resist the attempt to be involved in such activities.

It is crucial to assess employee commitment level since it is a key element in organizational success. Employers need to understand the level of employee's commitment to the Job, while employees need to be true with their commitment level since it contributes to the overall performance in the workplace.

Employees should focus on being committed to serve, set goals, stay inspired, look at the big picture, be accountable, stay the course, have a positive mindset and add value to the organization by making a positive impact. Committed employees are in high demand for excellent performance in the workplace. Employers do not have issues writing letters of recommendation for such employees whenever they need it.

Employers want to identify the best people, as great minds build great organizations. Committed people are ready to give their best to be successful. Employers need vast and versatile staff to drive the strategy.

Staff skill, intelligence, and reasoning especially technological innovation among many more can make or mar a business.

Chapter 6

Excellence On Point

...Employees must display excellence in the following skills: communication skills, time management skills, and administrative skills. Employees are required to use their initiative at all times...

Excellence is a state or quality of excelling. We need to build excellence into every area of our lives as a culture. Excellence comes from Consistent improvement; dedication to preparation. Practice yields increased excellence. Excellence is not a skill it is an attitude according to Ralph Matson.

Employees need to acquire excellent knowledge to succeed in the workplace. There is need for continuous innovation to positively transform, develop and sustain business excellence.

Set high standards in all areas of your life. Excellence is a gradual result of always striving to do better. Let your employer and people see the depth of your character and your spirit of excellence. Always strive for excellence, excel in your chosen pursuits, and raise the bar in excellence. Include excellence in all you do, be the best. Excellence should be your standard.

See yourself, as a Leader on your role, the first person to lead is yourself. Leadership is built on the foundation of character, not gifts or charisma. A leader's motive will determine his movement and mindset. If you don't stand for something, you will fall for anything. Be committed to excellence. Show empathy, communicate effectively and provide solutions. Excellence is attainable if only you are ready to pay the price. We live in a technology −driven age that demands digital literacy in nearly every profession. You must achieve excellence in the use of technology, computer skills, carrying out online research, and soft graphic skills. Make sure you go the extra mile to learn new skills, develop yourself.

Have a skill self-review in the following area to determine readiness for the Job: Complex problem solving skills; how prepared are you to solve complex problems? You may want to read more and seek information on problem solving skills, critical thinking, people management, coordinating with others, emotional intelligence, judgments and decision-making, service orientation.

Employability skills are what employers look out for in employees. This must be developed before applying for a Job. Add all these skills to your personal development plan while trying to get a job or immediately after.

Employees must display excellence in the following skills: communication skills, time management skills, and administrative skills. Employees are required to use their initiatives at all times. Remember you can never lose by taking action; you can only lose by not taking action. Be excellent in all you do in the workplace.

Employees should be accountable and responsible, courteous and helpful, equitable and consistent, knowledgeable and informative, efficient and responsive, professional and accessible.

An excellent employee is more observant, thinks more and understands in depth. The word of God says, "Whatever you do, work at it with all your heart, as working for the Lord, not for men." Excellent employees do and give their best to their employers.

When you put your whole heart into whatever you do, God will recognize it and bless you for it. You should strive and pursue excellence in all you do, for the sake of God; He blesses excellence.

Excellence is defined as the condition of surpassing standards of expectation. It is the dream of human resources (HR) practitioners for employees to achieve excellence in the workplace. To achieve people excellence, organizations need to focus on the growth and development of employees as well.

Keys to workplace excellence involves providing a compelling, positive vision with clear goals, communicate the right information at the right time, recognize and reward excellent performance and select the right person for the job.

Excellence is displayed by thinking ahead, communicating effectively, listen and take action, focus on solutions, under promise and over deliver, don't cut corners, meet deadlines, don't give up, ensure quality in all you do, do your best and give your best. Excellence comes from consistent improvement.

Employees with an excellent mindset generate higher productivity, higher morale, higher customer satisfaction and higher profits for their organizations.

Employers seek employees who are committed to excellence, always ready to do an outstanding job. We are in the age of excellence, do everything well, have a vision of high standards, be the best in your field, on your job and in your department. This comes from continuous learning and development, creativity and innovation. Have integrity tell and live the truth in everything you do. Do your part to create a better company, focus on delivering far more than is expected, be a role model from a behavioral perspective. Be excellent.

Be a person of excellence give your best. Have an excellent mindset. Your reputation is one of the most valuable things you have and it is built on the foundation of your personal integrity.

A person of integrity does the right thing when no one is watching. You can have talents, determination and vision, but without integrity you won't reach your full potential.
To live a life of excellence you must have standards. What is your standard in the area of moral ethics, integrity and discipline?

Do everything with excellence even if you need to back out from an organization; it should be done politely not aggressively as if you will never need them again.

Have an excellent mindset, tread with caution know that the bridge you burn now might be the one you will need to climb to your destination. No one knows tomorrow except God. Value and, build excellent relationships with those who come your path.

Chapter 7

What Employers Want

...An employer will consider you
because they need problems
solved not because you need a
job...

Employers want to identify the best people, great minds build great organizations. Employers want committed employees who are ready to give their best to the success of the organization.

Nigeria's labor market is seriously in hot competition for the unemployed youths. It's hereby critical for employees to really understand what their employers require from them to remain relevant on the Job and avoid getting fired.

An employer will consider you because they need problems solved not because you need a job. You must bear this in mind and know the value you will be adding to the company. You must have the required skills and competence to excel on the Job; employers are looking for smart brains with ideas. You must make use of your brain. You only get paid for bringing value to the marketplace; you must always innovate and be creative.

One must have a clear view of how you made your workplace better since you resumed. Be ready to exceed your employer's expectation by exceeding performance objective. Employers value critical thinkers and problem solvers. Employees who are passionate about success and are ready to do business the right way. Employees who are informed, prepared; smart and ready to perform exceptionally well on the Job

Employers look for skills, Intelligence, ability to reason in employees. Employers want people who can demonstrate competence, humility and integrity.

Employees must display Character, Competence, Conviction, Courage, Charisma, Commitment and Compassion. Employees who are ready to use their initiative are in high demand. Employees must demonstrate they have the skill and ability to perform on the role they are hired for; they have significant potential and demonstrate ability to learn quickly.

It is all about taking charge; you must have the right motivation to accomplish tasks on your own. By doing this, you display readiness and willingness to get things done without being asked or pushed.

Your relationship with your boss and colleagues can make or break your work experience. A healthy work relationship must be a top priority.

Employees should have a positive mindset. A positive mindset is infectious, and it spreads to others in the workplace. If you are a positive person, your job performance is usually better than that of a negative person because you are always looking for new ideas that yield higher productivity levels.

Employees must have good work habits, show up to work early be reliable, keep personal issues and work issues separate. Employees should keep driving productivity; productivity is the amount of work one produces in an hour, week, month or a year.

Employers would rather hire for Competency not necessary for degrees. Some employers care more about experience than education when hiring some skills cannot be learnt in the classroom. Experience is in demand rather than degrees. Employees are required to learn on the job to gain experience rather than focus on how much is being paid. Work to learn.

Develop yourself on the Job, be focused and learn. Knowledge gained on the job will be useful to you in future, creating more opportunities for you to establish your own business and be an employer of labor as well. God values your work, whatever you give in you take out.

Employers know that in looking for people to hire, you look for three qualities: Integrity, intelligence and energy. And if they do not have the first, the other two will kill you, according to Warren Buffet. It is hereby important for employers to focus on employing people high on integrity regardless of the competence, intelligence and skill level.

Integrity simply means the quality of being honest and having strong moral principles. The state of being whole and undivided. It is the practice of being honest, showing consistent and uncompromising adherence to strong morals, ethical principles and values.

In ethics, integrity is regarded as honesty and truthfulness or accuracy of one's actions. Employees with high integrity excel in the workplace. Honesty is an example of integrity in the workplace. Honesty encourages open communication between employers, employees and coworkers. It leads to effective relationships in an organization.

Employees who display integrity keep their word without excuses and without change of conditions, let your yes be yes and your no be no. They keep commitments, they avoid letting people down and notify people once commitment is likely to change.

Everyone makes mistakes, showing integrity means admitting to these mistakes and not being afraid to say, "I'm sorry I got it wrong". Words are powerful: it must be backed up with actions.

As the world merges into one global economy, human capital is more than ever, the key driver of profit and innovation. Results do not drive performance; results are the outcome of performance and people drive results reason employers must have the right employees in place to achieve results with outstanding performance.

Employers look out for employees who take pride in their job, give sincere and diligent service, have an excellent mindset, follows instructions, cheerful and helpful, does not look for shortcuts and honest. As employees getting a job should not be your key focus but how you will make the organization better because of your presence.

Be the best employee and give your best to your employer. I strongly believe one day you will move from being an employee to an employer of labor. When this happens you will expect same qualities from your employees and hope they understand what you want as an employer.

Congratulations! now you know what Employers want determine to be an Outstanding Employee.

Reflect

Are you ready to give your best to your Employer?

1

Can you clearly state what your Employer wants from you as an Employee?

2

What areas do you need to personally develop before getting a Job?

3

What values are you bringing to the Workplace

4

Can you boldly request a letter of recommendation from your former employer?

5

To seek further coaching and mentoring, kindly contact Bunmi Akingbade on:

08033325735 and 08153717008
Email: Lacare247@gmail.com
Facebook: Lacare innovative and creativity
Twitter: @Lacare247
Instagram: @Lacare247

Other books by the Author

- Love has Benefits
- Born for Greatness
- Greatness is in you (a book for children)
- The Shining Lady
- Think Nigeria

About the Book

Nigeria's labor market is seriously in hot competition for the unemployed youths. It is hereby critical for employees to really understand what their employers require from them to remain relevant on the Job.

Employers are considering you because they need problems solved not because you need a job. You must bear this in mind and know the value you will be adding to the company. You must have the required skills and competence to excel on the Job. Employers are looking for smart brains with ideas; you must make use of your brain. You only get paid for bringing value to the marketplace; you must always innovate and be creative.

"What Employers Want" is a must read guidebook for Job seekers, those already on the Job, Students and Employers of labor. The book provides the crucial foundation required for employees to excel in the workplace and understand what is expected from them. It also provides basic understanding to support employee's give their best to their employer at all times. Employers want to hire the right staff that will add value to the organization, you can be that employee.

About The Author

Bunmi Akingbade is out to deliver winning solutions that inspire a vibrant life; physically, spiritually and mentally. She has over 18 years corporate experience, a youth coach with over 16 years in the Youth Ministry cause of her with heartfelt passion for youths. She teaches principles and strategies that create personal growth.

She is the Founder of Lacare Help Ministry; Co-founder, Lacare Innovative and Creativity Initiative, a registered NGO in the Federal Republic of Nigeria, aimed at empowering youths to maximize their full potentials and build the nation by providing resources and training for their spiritual, personal, professional and business growth. She is a Speaker, Trainer and Consultant.

Married to Pastor Folorunsho Akingbade she's blessed with two wonderful children and many spiritual children.